SUCCESS
& WHAT IT COST

VOLUME 1

ANDRE ANTHONY LAVAIL JONES III

Copyright © 2023 Andre Anthony Lavail Jones III
All rights reserved. This publication, or any part thereof, may not be reproduced in any form or by any means, including electronic, photographic, or mechanical, or by any sound recording system, or by any device for storage and retrieval of information, without the written permission of the copyright owner.

Andre Anthony Lavail Jones III

This book is dedicated to you! I hope it motivates you to be the best version of yourself and put your all into whatever it is your heart desires.

TABLE OF CONTENTS

Introduction   7

Chapter 1
Procrastination: The Enemy Of Your Success   10

Chapter 2
Self-Discipline   17
- Importance Of Self-Discipline For Success   19

Chapter 3
Keep A Plan   22

Chapter 4
Sacrifice   28

Chapter 5
Taking Action   33

Chapter 6
The Company You Keep   38

Chapter 7
Trust The Process   44

Chapter 8
Patience   48
● Benefits Of Practicing Patience   51

Chapter 9
Identity/ Living In Your Truth   53

Chapter 10
Decisions   58
● 4 Things That Help Make Your Decisions Beneficial 64

Chapter 11
Seek God & Understanding   66

Conclusions   70

INTRODUCTION

Success is often defined as the achievement of desired visions and planned goals, whatever those goals may be. It is not necessarily a destination but a journey that helps develop the skills and resources you need to thrive.

There are many different tactics for how to be successful in life, but the strategy that works best for you may depend on what success means to you. If you think of success as doing well at work or earning a high salary, your professional goals and accomplishments will take priority.

While professional success can be one piece of the puzzle, it leaves out many other important areas of life. Family, romantic relationships, academics, and athletics are just a few areas where people may strive for success.

The only real limits on what you can do, have, or be are self-imposed. Once you make a clear, undeniable decision to change your life by casting off all your mental limitations and throwing your whole heart into the accomplishment of your goal, your ultimate personal success is virtually guaranteed, as long as you stay persistent.

In order to move the needle and achieve greater success, leaders must learn to follow a specific process wherein they master the art of thinking, planning, executing, and pivoting — in that order. Inner mastery helps you develop habits, attitudes, and beliefs that will enable you to live your life to the fullest. It allows you to develop the ability to fully control yourself in any situation without giving in to your whims.

Those with the deepest commitment to personal development and growth experience more opportunities and contributions. They often overcome patterns of frustration that cause most people to give up along the way. Incredible change happens in your life when you decide to take control of what you do have power over instead of craving control over what you don't.

Every winner is a story of dedication. Do you have a vision? Fix your eyes on the target and be ready to work really hard on it. Always remember there is no feast without a sacrifice. Nothing is free; everything has got a price, and you must be ready to pay it. But first, you must know what it will cost you.

CHAPTER 1

PROCRASTINATION:
THE ENEMY OF YOUR SUCCESS

" Procrastination is the thief of time. "

We all put things off until the last minute from time to time, but if it has become an entrenched behavior, it can be a sign that you need to get more focused. It's so easy to spend hours on something that has nothing to do with you personally or your goals. Many of us just can't stop scrolling down our Facebook newsfeeds, checking our text messages, or scrolling through TicTok. Although we are absolutely mesmerized by the digital age, it's truly taking up too much of our time and increasing our levels of procrastination. Procrastination is difficult to conquer because there are so many addictive distractions everywhere around us; however, it is vital to recognize why we are putting off important tasks that will hurt us in the long term.

Procrastination is an assassination of your career goals and dreams. It targets your brilliance and your potential until they are all but eliminated. Procrastination is designed to keep you just where you are because even by not making a decision, you are making a decision — a decision not to take action, and action is the only solution to get you back on track. When you procrastinate, you are putting off something you know that needs to be done. The more you put it off, the more anxious you feel because, at some level, you know you want to do it.

Procrastination stems from a fear of the outcome and a desire for perfection in getting tasks done, and it undermines you at every turn.

We are all guilty of procrastination at some point. Some

people allow it to sabotage them more than others, and it reflects in where they currently are in their lives. The good news is it's not too late to put an end to procrastination and begin to put in the work. The truth is, there's always something more interesting to do than the work at hand. The longer you put off your next level, the longer it will take to get there. We are all destined for greatness, but you have to be willing to go out into the world and make it happen! Procrastination is the enemy of success, and it will steal your dreams and your next level! You know what your next level consists of, and you know what actions you need to take to get there; you are only standing in the way of your own success by allowing procrastination to cripple your full potential.

I have found that people procrastinate for many reasons, as there are many types of procrastination a person may fall victim of. A few behavioral types of procrastination are the perfectionist, the dreamer, the worrier, the crisis-maker, and the overdoer.

Perfectionists are the ones who pay too much attention to minor details. A perfectionist is afraid to start the task at hand because they get stressed about getting every detail right. They can also get stuck in the process, even when they've started, because they're too scared to move on.

The perfectionist would be someone who puts off finishing a task due to their worry of not getting every single detail perfect. Instead of letting your obsession with details take up all your time, and cause you to overthink, be clear about the purpose of your tasks and create deadlines for each to overcome this type of procrastination. This will force you to stay focused and finish your task within the time frame. Remember, it's ok to pay attention to details, but it's not like it has to be perfect unless you're building a bridge. Your ideas will never be perfect enough to please everyone.

The dreamer, in contrast, is someone who enjoys making the ideal plan more than taking action. They are highly creative but find it hard to actually finish a task. The dreamer doesn't like details. This makes ideas difficult to implement. The dreamer would be someone who comes up with really dope ideas but can't begin to tell you how they will bring the ideas to life, which causes them to never even begin. Dreaming is good, but keep in mind, you must have a plan of execution to use as your blueprint.

The worriers are scared to take on tasks they think they can't manage. They would rather put off work than be judged by others when they make mistakes. The worriers have an excessive need for security, causing them to fear risk. They fear change, causing them to avoid finishing projects so they don't have to leave the comfort of the "known." The worrier is so anxious they ask themselves 'what if' a lot. They're cautious. Because of that, they're afraid to step down and actually do what needs to be done. If you are this type of procrastinator, set a goal and break down the plan into small tasks that you can take action on right away.

The crisis-maker deliberately pushes back work until the last minute. They find deadlines exciting and believe that they work best when working under pressure, which causes them to manage their time poorly. The 'Crisis Maker' believes that in order to be motivated to do a task, they need the stress or pressure that is inherent in last-minute action. Without this, they believe they won't perform at their best. They need pressure to alleviate the boredom. There is an issue with this. If you compare the quality of work when started at the last minute and when started within a reasonable timeframe, which do you think will give better results? Spend your morning working on what you find the most challenging. This will give you a sense of achievement, and it will help you build momentum for a productive day ahead. Try to break down your tasks into smaller sub-tasks.

Understand how much time and energy is needed for a given task, and make realistic calculations. Being forced to rush the work because you will perform better is just an illusion because it leaves you no room for reviewing the work to make it better afterward.

The Over-Doer finds it difficult to prioritize and say no to things, which results in too many demands being made on their time. They take on too much and then procrastinate because they feel overwhelmed and simply have too much to do. The Over-Doer should acknowledge their limitations and try not to take on too many tasks, learning to say no to tasks where necessary. They should also prioritize their tasks, so they're only tackling one task at a time and make a daily to-do list to help them maintain these priorities.

If you are someone who suffers from procrastination, my advice to you would be to set goals, then work towards them, and also routinely re-examine them. If you have concrete goals and dreams of success, you will feel more motivated than people who drift along aimlessly.

Write your goals down. Research shows that writing down your goals increases your chances of sticking to them by 42%. Then track and measure your progress on your journey to success, knocking out milestones along the way. When you get into the office each day, you must know exactly what you want to achieve. To help you set goals, imagine what you want and work towards it. Where do you see yourself in one, two, or even ten years' time? Set yourself targets that must be hit along the way to your eventual goal. Break things down, and remember, success is a process.

CHAPTER 2

| **SELF DISCIPLINE** |

The single most important attribute to becoming successful is self-discipline. It helps you stay focused on reaching your goals, gives you the courage to stick with difficult tasks, and allows you to overcome obstacles and discomfort as you push yourself to new heights.

What exactly is self-discipline? It's the ability to control your impulses, emotions, reactions, and behaviors; it allows you to forego short-term gratification in favor of long-term satisfaction and gain. It's saying "no" when you want to say "yes." It isn't about leading a restrictive and boring life void of enjoyment—it's next to impossible to be self-disciplined in all areas of your life. Rather than attempting to be disciplined in all you do, use it to focus on what's most important.

The 'self' in self-discipline means you have the willpower to do these things on your own, without someone telling you to do them. So self-discipline means you control your feelings and even do hard things so you can be better and have more prosperity. More than one self-discipline definition can help us understand the concept better, though. Consider these dictionary definitions:

According to Oxford Languages Dictionary, Self-discipline is "the ability to control one's feelings and overcome one's weaknesses; the ability to pursue what one thinks is right despite temptations to abandon it.

IMPORTANCE OF SELF-DISCIPLINE FOR SUCCESS

When you learn and master self-discipline, some magical things start to happen. For example:

Self-Discipline Boosts Your Work Ethic

The great thing about success is that it builds on itself. When you experience success, it's addicting. You automatically want more success. In this way, self-discipline increases your work ethic. The late Jim Rohn, who was a leading expert and scholar of success, often pointed out that one discipline nearly always leads to another discipline.

You Will Have a Higher Self-Esteem

There is nothing that boosts your self-esteem more than completing a goal or creating an accomplishment. When you're self-disciplined, you will have far more accomplishments in your life, and you will grow to have higher self-esteem.

It Helps You Get Stuff Done

The key to success is getting high-value things done and self-discipline is what helps you get things done. As human beings, we're biologically engineered to look for shortcuts because shortcuts are efficient. Unfortunately, this means that most of us have to make a concerted effort to get up every day and tackle the hard things.

Self-Discipline Creates Habits

Anytime you can put some areas of your life on autopilot, you're freeing up time and energy to do the hard things. When you create habits, you're building self-discipline in your life. Habits makes it easy to stay on track, and self-discipline creates habits.

Being Disciplined Helps You Focus

More than ever, we live in a world that is full of distractions. When you have self-discipline, you are more likely to stay focused on your goals. No one except Mark Zuckerberg ever became successful by being on Facebook all day, and honestly, we doubt he spends all of his time watching kitten videos and posting photos of what he had for lunch.

Self-Discipline Helps You Achieve Mastery

How do you master anything? You have to spend a lot of time practicing and doing. Experts such as Malcolm Gladwell suggest that to master something, you need to spend about 10,000 hours doing it. This can only happen if you're self-disciplined.

You Realize Your Full Potential

Do human beings have unlimited potential? In a way, we do. However, we're limited by the number of days we have on this earth and the number of hours in the day. Keep this in mind: uber-successful people like Oprah Winfrey, Jeff Bezos, and Elon Musk all have the same number of hours in the day as the rest of us.

CHAPTER 3

| **KEEP A PLAN** |

〰〰〰〰〰〰〰〰〰〰〰〰

Another ingredient that is absolutely crucial to success is planning.

Planning is setting goals, developing strategies as well as outlining tasks and schedules to accomplish the goals. *It is the process of deciding in detail how to do something before you actually start to do it.* Success doesn't come from luck. The most successful people didn't just get lucky; they had a strategic success plan and then executed it. Whether you have business goals to accomplish or personal goals you want to tackle, achieving them starts with a well-written plan. If you don't have a plan, you will be stumbling around working on tasks that don't really matter, hoping to magically become successful. Again, success does not happen by magic. It takes hard work and discipline, and with some advance planning, you'll be equipped with everything you need to begin that work. Success comes to those who plan for it.

When you create a plan, the likelihood that you will be successful skyrockets. Your plan will act as your roadmap to success. Once you've created a plan, you will know exactly what you need to do in order to be successful and how you're going to do it. It maps out your overall strategy to reach your ideal goal. How could you find your way to your destination if you have no idea where you're even going in the first place? Having a plan helps you focus your efforts on initiatives that align with your goals. In order to achieve your goals, you must develop a plan that determines what direction you should be heading before you start your engines and head out to nowhere.

When you achieve your success a lot earlier than other people, they are likely to say you are lucky. But only you know better and how hard you have worked to attain such heights in a short period of time. You know you have increased your probability to succeed by taking calculated risks, working very hard, dealing successfully with big and small problems, and overcoming the many problems and difficulties which you see as feedback but other people see as failures and quit (you faced the storm and overcame). It is this combination of actions plus perseverance and endurance over a period of time that makes your eventual success inevitable. It has got nothing to do with luck. Over every mountain, there is always a path, although it will not be seen from the valley; people think you are lucky because what they see are your successes. They only see outside the wall but never know what goes on behind the scenes and what it took to get where you are. Success in life is not about luck, but it's about managed thoughts, focused attention, and calculated actions.

Studies show that without a plan, we do what's passive and easy, not what brings real progress. The biggest impediment to maintaining a high output is not being clear on what you want to work on next. You can plan to do high-value tasks every day, exercise, eat healthily, help someone, practice gratitude, learn a new skill, etc. It helps you stay focused and avoid the many distractions that come your way every day. Simultaneously you can plan for downtime to take a vacation, go for a walk, spend time with family, etc. Just imagine what you could achieve by just planning ahead and committing to those plans. For a productive life, plan ahead; it's the best way to be sure you don't overlook anything important.

There are three overall plans that you need to be successful. They will help you compartmentalize your goals and move you from one area to the next with more confidence, focus, and speed. Each plan builds on the other and strengthens them.

#1 Life Plan

This is your overall purpose and goals in life. This is a big, macro look at what you want out of life. What do you want in your career? For your family? For your life? For your health?

This is the plan that gets you closer to a completed cycle of action toward your goals, targets, and dreams. The thoughts you think control everything, and you need to focus them on the right trajectory for your life. One little shift in your thinking can create a mental trigger that drives new actions. Affirming what is possible on a daily basis creates the motivation to act.

#2 Sales Plan

This is how you attack the marketplace. This is the plan that makes all other plans possible. It feeds everything else. If you have a bulletproof sales plan, it will help you achieve your life plan. The goal is not to work for someone forever but to use the job you work for as a stepping stone to fund your business and help you get closer to where you are headed in life. A lot of people spend 20 to 30 years with the same sales plan without changing it. If you learn to produce, then you can do anything.

#3 Day Plan

What do you need to do every day to create your life and sales plan? What are you going to do today? Write it down. Every time you write out your day, you'll have more direction and certainty. Planning your day gives you control over it. This then leads to control over your customers or contacts, which equals income. And this strengthens your sales plan.

You have to take responsibility for your life by planning it. Using these three plans will create certainty in your life, which leads to more confidence. When you are confident, you feel motivated -- and that's when you stop thinking and take action. Success is a process. Follow the steps and put in the work.

SACRIFICE

*S*acrifice is the surrender of something valuable for the sake of something better.

> *I hated every minute of training, but I said, 'Don't quit. Suffer now and live the rest of your life as a champion.'*
>
> **– Muhammed Ali**

No matter what goals or aspirations you might have, one thing is certain: There is a price you must pay to get what you want in life. In fact, there is no sidestepping the fact that any type of success demands something from you. It's simply the way life works, and rarely will a shortcut ever get you there. Now, this rule pertains to sacrifice. It's the realization that you may need to give up something you have now which is of value in order to attain something greater in the future.

The great thing about sacrifice is that it is temporary. By sacrificing for your goals, you are temporarily giving up one thing for the long-term success of another thing. To put it into perspective, let's say that you are a boxer training for the biggest fight of your career. It will be mandatory that you change your diet to be in the best shape possible for this fight and stay at the weight you are supposed to be. After you've won the fight, you can certainly go back to your old eating habits, but until then, you must make that sacrifice.

Something about me that you might not know unless you know me personally is that I love to shop, I love to eat, and I also enjoy stepping out and having a good time. However, I came to the realization that unnecessary shopping can wait because I need to save more. I had to cut back on eating out because I realized those $20/$25 meals 2-3 times a week add up! I can save an extra $50-$75 a week by going to the grocery store and grabbing food to cook for my household. As much as I would enjoy stepping out to have a good time, I realized that could wait until I get where I'm going. Let's be completely honest with ourselves; a good night out can easily cost you $100 plus. I had to make these sacrifices because I understood how much money was being wasted that could have gone towards saving. This is the mindset we must have when seeking greatness. By sacrificing the present, you can mold and manipulate your future reality.

By forming this kind of mindset, one can actually gain time. Maybe not actual time, but leisure time. Instead of using their free time to make themselves happy with frivolous things that the individual doesn't actually gain anything from, they use their time to work towards a meaningful and rewarding goal. This way, when they reach the pinnacle of success early in their life, they no longer have to worry about working a nine-to-five job to make ends meet. They have all the time in the world to do whatever it is they want to do, so they did indeed gain time on the backend.

Society today tries to deny the law of sacrifice at every turn, promising people that they can fulfill their desires without having to forsake anything at all. "Lose weight without giving up your favorite foods!" "Get ripped without long workouts!" "Get rich without having to work hard!" The fantasy that you can have whatever you'd like without ever paying for it is an incredibly seductive fantasy. But it is only a fantasy. There is always a price to pay. If you want the nice things in life, you have to work hard and save your money. Sure, sometimes fame and good fortune seemingly drop into someone's lap. The law of sacrifice is not as irrevocable as, say, the law of gravity. But as Frederick Douglass said: **"A man, at times, gets something for nothing, but it will, in his hands, amount to nothing".** See the cases of folks who win the lottery and then squander it all away.

This is the beauty of the law of sacrifice. Not only is it the only path to achieving your goals, but the path itself prepares you to handle life at the top. Sacrificing not only gets you to your goals but hones and shapes you along the way.

The denial of the law of sacrifice keeps a man from progressing in life. To reach your goals, you must move forward, which necessitates leaving some things behind. Quote me on this, every successful person has had to give up something they wanted to do because they knew there was something of greater value that they had to accomplish. Here's the thing, though. The things that look like sacrifices on the front end are actually investments when you look at them in hindsight. You give away something upfront, but the reward you get is worth much more than what you gave up in the first place. That's the good old boring delayed gratification for the win.

CHAPTER 5

TAKING ACTION
KNOWLEDGE + ACTION = SUCCESS

"Action is the foundational key of all success." —
Pablo Picasso

It is easier to direct a moving vehicle than one that is parked. So, why not keep moving? Your actions encourage what you don't see to become visible as you go through the intentional motions.

Actions create habits – which lead to success

The more you do something, the easier it is to keep doing it, whether good or bad. You cannot succeed if you do nothing. By maintaining the action, you are setting yourself up for a greater chance of hitting your goals.

When we commit to raising our standards, we begin to expect more from ourselves. We demand better outcomes and become willing to do the hard work. By raising our expectations, we form new habits. When we turn our "should" into "must," and our "maybe" into "absolutely," real change occurs. Accountability requires persistent follow-through, ultimately creating new habits. It goes beyond talk and pushes us into action.

This change isn't easy. Old habits die hard, and new habits are even harder to form. When we finally expect more from ourselves, we commit to hard work that leads to permanent habits. Those habits cut through the noise, become noticed, and command respect. Those habits generate influence and create credibility among those who surround you.

Actions facilitate the method of elimination

How will you know if what you are doing will get you down the lane of success? Trial and error.

You cannot eliminate what doesn't work and establish what does work except through trial and error. You miss 100% of the shots you don't take. That requires action on your part.

You have to be ready and willing to test in real-time to understand the complexity of what you are going after. The more action you take, the deeper your possibilities grow. If you want to escape the world of mediocrity, you have to embrace the power of taking action. By doing so, you keep moving in the right direction.

Action Utilizes Knowledge

Reading and learning is very important. You must gather all the necessary information needed for your success journey. However, no matter how much you read or learn, you will not become successful unless you take action and apply the proper information. It's easy to get stuck in research and making sure everything is going to play out as planned. But you can get buried in the preparation and forget that to get you moving to the next level, you must take action. Doing the work may not be so exciting. In fact, action can be tedious, especially if you don't get the desired results. Yet, knowledge can lead your action when utilized appropriately. Don't sit on what you know. Knowledge is power ONLY when applied!

I began to write this book during my time in prison; however, it took me a year and a half after my release to take action and complete it. Although I knew the information, even had already begun the writing process, it meant nothing if I never took the action to finish and publish.

Failure to take action can stem from many areas, the main one being the failures that have already occurred. Look at your failures as a lesson learned, so you can be willing to learn even more. Stretching yourself beyond what you can see builds trust within yourself and seizes the opportunity of the present!

If you're struggling to get something started or completed, identify the essential, actionable steps and get started comfortably.

Make the first few steps so easy you won't fail to start. Whether you're trying to learn a new language, read more books, get more exercise, or accomplish any other self-improvement goal, the key is a daily or weekly schedule that helps you make progress consistently.

One glass of water a day. One extra vegetable. Three pushups. One sentence of writing a day. Two minutes of meditation. This is how you start a habit that lasts.

Remember the importance of small actions. They're the building blocks in the architecture of your life, the quiet victories you win for yourself each day.

There is no need to put off till tomorrow what you can do today. Build consistency in doing something with intention, and see how your life changes. If you wait for the right time to show up, you will be waiting forever. Take your day into your own hands and create your "now."

Cheers to you for taking action and demanding success in this new season of your life! The best is yet to come.

CHAPTER 6

THE COMPANY YOU KEEP

"**In Proverbs 13:20,** Solomon, the wise guy, wrote: *"He that walketh with wise men shall be wise: but a companion of fools shall be destroyed."*

1 Corinthians 15:33 - Do not be deceived: *"Bad company corrupts good morals."*

Help me grow, or watch me go.
Iron sharpens iron.

Did you know you are an average of the five people you spend the most time with? One of the most important decisions we make in life is who we choose to be around. In fact, there is an old proverb that reads, "Show me your friends, and I'll tell you who you are". We must be cautious about whom we surround ourselves with because of the short and long-term effects. People are like sponges. We absorb the energy that surrounds us. If our environment is happy most of the time, enjoying and focusing on the pleasant things in life, it'll be easier for us to feel happy. The same would happen in reverse. Surrounded by grumpy and miserable people, it'd be difficult for us to keep smiling. It's just like your mother always told you: be careful who you hang around; be careful who you associate with; guard who pours into your life. Don't let just anyone come in and start placing things or speaking things into your life. Guard your heart. Guard your mind. Guard your soul. Why? Because evil communications corrupt good manners. They corrupt good actions. They corrupt the right mindset. They change the way we interact with those around us.

We all have goals in our lives, but which objectives are a must? The pursuits you choose to invest time in are a reflection of your standards, and so are your relationships. Are you trying to grow? If so, then why would you choose to hang around people who bring negativity and distraction into your life? Surrounding yourself with good people can affect every aspect of your life, from business to romantic relationships. When you surround yourself with positivity, you're more likely to adopt empowering beliefs and see life as happening for you instead of to you. Just as you benefit when you surround yourself with people who make you happy, you suffer when those in your business or social circles are negative or narrow-minded.

Surround yourself with the dreamers and the doers, the believers and thinkers, but most of all, surround yourself with those who see greatness within you, even when you don't see it yourself.

You truly are as good as the company you keep. As you go through life, you begin to realize how important having true friends really is. Navigating your 20s is a difficult and confusing time and one better traveled with wholesome, close friends by your side. Unfortunately, as we go through this time, we realize the people we once counted on are no longer the people we once thought they were.

The type of people you surround yourself with speaks of your values and what you stand for. We have all heard of the concept of being guilty by association, the act of people associating your behaviors and thoughts with the people you hang out with. If one of your friends acts in a negative way, you will be lumped in with him or her. Whether it is true or not, it is all based on perception. Regardless if you believe yourself to be a strong-minded individual, a time may come when your bad company starts to influence your good behavior or even cost you your success, freedom, and in many cases, your life.

It is better to be alone than in the wrong company. Tell me who your best friends are, and I will tell you who you are. If you run with wolves, you will learn how to howl, but if you associate with eagles, you will learn how to soar to great heights. People perceive you based on the actions the people closest to you display. They make the assumption that people who are similar will spend time together. While you may be better than the company you keep, it does send a signal to those who do not know you well enough to make their own judgments. If you spend time with people who treat you poorly, this gives off the impression that you lack self-respect. Whether you like it or not, you will be judged based on the people you associate with.

Who are your friends? Who do you clique with on a daily basis? What are they adding to your life? Or, should I say, what are they taking away from your life? Is your relationship with them profitable to your soul and your future?

Identifying the people in your life who are bringing you down is the first step in making shifts to your peer group or colleagues. Letting go of negative relationships will allow you more time to surround yourself with successful people.

When you decide that you are going to take total and complete control of your personal and professional destiny, you need sunlight. Negative people bring darkness. You need people in your inner circle who are doing things, going places, and moving upward and forward, not backward. If you want to jumpstart a new career, a new job, or a new life, then you have to be the driver of your own success bus. As the driver, you determine who gets on the bus and where they will sit on your bus, and you determine who gets off the bus. Negative people will keep their foot on the brake and prevent you from moving forward or going anywhere. Positive people have their foot on the gas, and they will drive you to new places that will ensure a successful arrival at your destination.

CHAPTER 7

| **TRUST THE PROCESS** |

Life is a marathon, not a sprint.
Slow & Steady wins the race.

Life shows how steady-paced consistency and efforts that are compounded produce better results. Too often, people believe that significant changes happen quickly, but that is rarely the case. In fact, life is much more of a marathon than a sprint. This idiom tells us that life thrives on small moments, and it takes consistent, thoughtful training and decision-making to do well.

Being impatient while the law of process is at work can cause you to look at someone else's lane and desire theirs because it looks smoother and easier instead of submitting to your own process. Don't be deceived; everyone must go through their own process. And, of course, if there is an attempt to skip, you will be unprepared and exposed when it's time for the rubber to meet the road.

When you take strides on purpose while submitting to your process, you develop something valuable to bring to the world. You see, although the world awaits your gifts and talents, character, along with courage and resilience, can only be formed through the law of process. Then, your purposeful strides will cause you to be around for the long haul.

A lot of us have fell victim to not trusting in our process. Nowadays, since we are able to watch one another's day-to-day lives through social media, everyone wants to be like the next person instead of following their own paths. What people don't understand is although it may seem as if someone has gotten to where they are by luck or by doing a few easy tasks to get to a place in life where they have everything that they may want, they still had to go through the process. Behind the scenes, people fail time and time again, but they will only show their victories. The fantasy of you following in their footsteps and getting the exact same results will always result in your disappointments. We see this more than often, with everyone wanting to pursue rap careers. They see someone's rising and figure, "I can do that too". We must all search for our own purpose in life and follow our own significant paths to reap the fruits of our labor. We must eliminate the idea of us magically hitting the instant success button. The truth is instant success does not exist. It is only a fantasy.

To trust the process means to remain committed. It means showing up every day, despite the challenges, and not always seeing progress. Rushing the process typically leads to negative experiences. I have seen this firsthand and have most certainly experienced it personally. I dedicated my late teen to hustling, thinking I could speed up my success if I made some quick money. However, that mindset actually set me back more than anything. You can have 366 good days for that one day to go bad and set you back years. We have to pace ourselves—if we try to go too fast, we are more likely to make a mistake that could cost us the race. The correct mindset we must adopt is slow and steady wins the race. Consistency will overall be more beneficial than being hasty or careless just to get something done, even if your progress is slow! Slow motion is better than no motion! Period.

When we allow life to reveal itself to us, we live in the present moment, knowing that we are exactly where we are supposed to be. Unfortunately, a lot of people jump too far forward. In their desire to reach their final destination, they forget about the journey. Unfortunately, life and comfort don't co-exist. In today's world, nothing is permanent, and at any moment, life could throw you a curveball that could change the game. When you trust the process, you accept and have faith in the unknown. You step outside of your comfort zone and allow life to guide you along your journey. Let go of fear and stop trying to control life. Anything worth having in life will not come easy, and anything that comes easy won't last long. The only way to practically guarantee a definite arrival at your destination is that you must trust in the process. It will be worth it in the end.

Success & What it Costs

CHAPTER 8

| **PATIENCE** |

atience is the strength of will to navigate the obstacles and the challenges that may come your way as you go through the process. Patience is essential because there will be problems. There will be people who irritate you and situations that frustrate you. If you are patient, you stay focused on doing the work.

Stop searching for the instant button. Success isn't instant. This is exactly why people fail over and over again – they expect instant results. If you go to the gym for a month, you can be easily discouraged when your dream body isn't staring back at you in the mirror. So, you give up. But remember, those seemingly insignificant actions build over time. You can't see the results from these actions in five days, five weeks, or even five months. It's not until the summation of all of those small actions over time – all of those workouts over the course of a year – produce an end result that the drastic difference is realized.

We're told from a very early age that patience is a virtue. However, very few of us are ever really shown or taught how to be patient. Patience is something we consciously do. Patience is like any other hard-earned discipline: The more we practice it, the more patient we become.

Whatever it is you want to achieve in life, one of the important keys to getting there is having patience. It is something that will keep you on track despite that struggles or bad situations that may come your way. Patience is the key to success in life. You must be patient, especially if what you chase is something worth having.

The accomplishment that you want to have might be something that comes in months or, in most cases, years. During that time, there will be constant thoughts of giving up. You might wonder how much longer you must suffer yourself. You may think about whether it is even worth it. Whether the road that you travel will lead you to what you want in life.

You may keep improving and find better ways as you keep on moving forward. However, the last thing you want to do is stop trying. The moment that you decide to quit will be the moment that you fail to succeed.

It took me to go to prison to realize how important patience was. For one, your time is not yours in the penitentiary. You are on the officer's time. Once I came to the realization that I could make my time much harder, feeling as if the guards were there to make my stay easier is when it all clicked. Your visit <u>begins at 2:30</u>, but it's <u>2:35</u>. "Where the hell is the guard? Let me bang on the door until they come" is the wrong idea. I had to learn to be patient. Patience stuck with me after prison because I was able to apply that same mindset to life and my goals. Everything won't happen in your timing, and that is ok, and that does not mean it won't happen for you in the next few months or years. Patience takes strength of will to keep pushing through your many challenges until you make it through the process.

BENEFITS OF PRACTICING PATIENCE

When we lack patience, we are unable to delay gratification for more than the moment, which fills us with frustration. Frustration is the emotional energy that drives "quitting." When we're impatient, we're unable to work toward our business goals in a dedicated fashion. We start to quit to start again, and we run this pattern over and over.

Successful people set themselves apart from the rest of the pack by mastering the skill sets which lead to success. Patience gives us courage. It gifts us the ability to work steadily toward our goals. And when we reach our goals consistently, we build our reputation. Great reputations are developed through persevering and not giving up, which stem from having the patience needed to make it to the finish line.

Patience puts us in direct control of ourselves. And there is no more powerful aid to success than self-possession. When we are patient, we give ourselves time to choose how to respond to a given event, rather than get emotionally hijacked by our emotions. It allows us to stay gathered no matter what is happening. With self-management, we build trust in our capacity to deal with whatever comes our way.

Patience increases our threshold of tolerance. It gives us the foresight to expect obstacles on our path and to deal with them diplomatically. When we expect challenges, we respond with more courage, strength, and optimism. We understand that emotional discomfort is a part of any obstacle and accept that life's curveballs are a natural part of the business cycle; therefore, we don't add any additional suffering, bitterness, or revenge to the mix. Instead, we roll up our sleeves and do the work we need to do.

Patience brings hope. It brings a continued renewal of belief in our desired goals and in the heights we are striving to achieve. When we are hopeful, we have a natural resilience and willingness to keep trying because we trust in the process.

Any endeavor that could potentially become a great success requires us to dedicate ourselves to a long, hard effort. This is only a possibility when we are patient with our progress and truly trust in our process, no matter how long it takes.

CHAPTER 9

IDENTITY/LIVING IN YOUR TRUTH

Self-awareness is one of the most important realizations a person must have. I know you already have an idea of who you desperately want to be, but it may not be who you were designed to be. When you know who you truly are within, you will finally see where you and your specific gifts fit into the bigger picture. When you discover who you are, you will spend less time spinning your wheels. Self-awareness also allows you to become more goal-oriented. If you are not aware of your own passion, interests, thoughts, actions, behaviors, and mood patterns, then it will be tough to be able to understand the world around you.

Knowing what's important to you is central to your career journey. To develop career ideas and explore the next steps, you need to better understand your interests, values, strengths, and skills and how they relate to meaningful work and the life you want to lead. Once you have a clear understanding and become aware of your own passion, interests, behaviors, and mood patterns, you'll have a better understanding of the world around you. Knowing your true identity puts you one step closer to living in your divine purpose.

I spend 2018 to 2020 in the department of corrections. During that time, I was able to take a step back and examine who I really was. I found myself digging as far as preschool because I needed answers. Who am I? What do I stand for? What morals do I obtain? What is my purpose? How did my life get to that point where I was? I felt lower than I ever had during that time. But what I needed to know was who I was in and out without the influence of friends, family, or anyone else, for that matter. That would explain why I was where I ended up and how I would get to my turning point. It would also reveal what changes I needed to apply to get the best results out of my life. After not even too much digging, I noticed patterns in my life. Then I was able to identify who I truly was on the inside. Without me discovering who I was, I would not have been able to get to where I am physically and mentally today.

As we grow up, our beliefs, emotions, and behavior are shaped as well as changed with social interaction, which happens on day to day basis either directly (friends, family) or indirectly (media). This social interaction thus leads to social influence, which is defined as the effect of other people on our attitude.

Very few people understand exactly who they are. We live in a world where everything is instant, and time for reflection is rare—and for most of us, we don't have much spare time for deep analysis and reflection. But the fact that we're distracted doesn't take away from the importance of discovering who we are.

When you become self-aware, you will spend less time spinning your wheels. I reflect on my past because it allows me to appreciate how far I've come. But when I do, I always think of the many years of dead time I wasted hustling, dealing with certain people (friends & relationships) that really served my life no purpose. I realized that what I was doing was spinning my wheels, but I wasn't getting anywhere. This is the case in a lot of people's lives. Consider the image of a car stuck in the mud. Without traction, its tires spin, but the car doesn't move—it is still stuck. The car is expending a lot of energy but not moving forward. Without a change in the situation, the car will continue to be stuck in the mud. Hence, the metaphor commonly used when a person or group is very busy but accomplishing very little is "spinning their wheels." Often, they are blind to the fact that they are spinning their wheels because they are so preoccupied with doing what they consider as busy work.

Although those years of my life had a major effect in getting me to that turning point from all the lessons, being self-aware allowed me to make critical changes so that I could get aligned with the tasks I was put on earth to accomplish.

Your identity **defines your relationship with yourself and determines the relationship with everything else in your life**: money, business, people, failure, success, etc. It becomes your way of being. Your identity will determine how you show up in your business or job and life as a whole. Examining yourself requires constant self-awareness and self-consciousness. This, in turn, **shapes how you interact with others and can lead to deeper, more fruitful relationships**. It also frees you from the expectations of others, allowing you to be your authentic self. Underneath the exterior, and all the labels, ideas, and preferences—is you. Understanding who exactly that person is can help build your confidence. Uncovering your identity takes time and effort, but it plays a major role in your overall success. You will be in tune with who you are and what you believe, and you'll be free to live more consciously and purposefully, which leads to success.

Use your reflections to fight your biggest fears because when you understand who you are, your purpose will finally become bigger than your fears. Focusing on your strengths gives you the needed traction to make a bigger and better difference in the world. When you know yourself, you will find more peace, and you will find success quicker than ever before.

CHAPTER 10

| DECISIONS |

> *" There is a choice you have to make in everything you do. So keep in mind that in the end, the choice you make, makes you. "*
>
> ~ John Wooden

We not only make decisions, we are made by them. Every one of us is where we are today as a result of the decisions we made yesterday. I have seen this firsthand. Life has shown me time and time again the importance of decision-making. I've been blessed to learn not only from my experiences but from the experiences of those close to me. I have friends that were killed in the streets growing up due to the choices they made. I have a really close friend of mine, Travis, serving 80 years in prison right now due to choices he made in his teens! The crazy part is Travis was a good dude, never was a street guy, and always had dreams. However, good decision-making must be applied daily because one wrong decision can be the last you ever get to make on your own! Decisions powerfully shape our lives, and the effects of one major decision can linger for years or can even last for a lifetime.

Most people do not realize that every major decision leads to a chain of events we cannot accurately predict. Those chains of events can be positive or negative. If we make good decisions, the outcomes should be positive; if we make poor choices, the outcomes can be negative. Everything in our lives is a choice, even doing nothing. At any moment, we have hundreds of decision-making options, some significant and some seemingly insignificant. We need to become more aware of our decision-making process. Too often, we operate on autopilot, doing things by habit rather than by making conscious decisions. Life is a series of decisions, and as we realize this, we can slow the process down and recognize that what we are doing is making a conscious decision instead of falling back on habit and past poor decisions.

Successful people approach decisions differently; they have a methodical way of looking at choices. More than just a choice in the moment, good decision-making takes discipline. Although there are many strategies successful people use for effective decision-making, these are practices that most successful people apply and benefit greatly from. Consider these the cream of the crop.

Decision-making works like a muscle: As you use it over the course of the day, it gets too exhausted to function effectively. One of the best strategies successful people use to work around their decision fatigue is to eliminate smaller decisions by turning them into routines. Doing so frees up mental resources for more complex decisions. Steve Jobs famously wore a black turtleneck to work every day. Mark Zuckerberg still dons a hoodie. Both men have stated that these iconic images are the simple result of daily routines intended to cut down on decision fatigue. They were both aware of their finite daily ability to make good decisions, just like Barack Obama, who said, "You'll see I wear only gray or blue suits. I'm trying to pare down decisions. I don't want to make decisions about what I'm eating or wearing because I have too many other decisions to make."

The following are some of the practices that successful people have incorporated into their lives that distinguish them from every other person.

Successful people pay attention to their emotions.

It is very important to recognize when your ability to make good decisions are vulnerable, such as when you're in a hurry, prideful, angry, lonely, rejected, or tired. Successful people know when they're not in a good place to make a decision, and they say, "Let me sleep on that or let me think about that. I'll get back to you." They're okay with not giving immediate answers. They defer until they know their mind's right.

Make big decisions in the morning.

When you're facing a stream of important decisions, a great trick is to wake up early and work on your most complicated tasks before you get hit with a bunch of distracting minor decisions (phones ringing, emails coming in) and things of that sort. A similar strategy is to do some of the smaller things the night before to get a head start on the next day. For instance, lay out your outfit at night, so you don't even have to think about it when you wake up.

Use Exercise to Recharge

One thing that most successful people have in common is an uncompromising attitude toward fitness and exercise. This is because fitness can instill in you the fundamental building blocks necessary for achieving success. Focusing on physical fitness actually paves the way for mental fitness to ensue. Not only does it create space for mental clarity, but it also develops the connection between your mind and body. Through fitness, you can push past your comfort zone and self-imposed limits to find that the limit actually does not exist. As you crush your fitness goals, surpassing what you never thought possible, you will realize that the obstacles in your life are no different and that as long as you keep progressing, nothing is out of reach. In addition, fitness builds a fundamental knowledge base of the mindset you must cultivate in order to achieve anything that seems out of reach.

Evaluate Opinions Objectively

Successful people weigh their options against a predetermined set of criteria because they know that this makes decision-making easier and more effective. "How does this decision benefit me? How does it hurt me? Does the decision reflect my values? Would I regret making this decision? Would I regret not making this decision?".

4 THINGS THAT HELP MAKE YOUR DECISIONS BENEFICIAL

1. **Action**—a choice means nothing without action behind it. Whatever you decide to do, do it.

2. **Timing**—making the right choice at the right time increases your odds of success; don't wait to do something you know you need to do.

3. **Management**—revisit your decisions and make sure you're living up to them.

4. **Acceptance**—this comes down to three things: ownership, authenticity, and accountability; be responsible for your choices, invite others to speak about them, and keep the commitments public to ensure you stay on track.

Remember, everything you do and everything you are is the end result of a decision. Decisions are merely steps or milestones in the course of our lives. All decisions are sequential and cumulative—each succeeding decision builds upon the previous many, and there's no end to the process. Life is full of tough choices, but they don't need to be massive drains on your time. Lay a strong foundation to make decisions generally, and you'll spend less time agonizing over your decisions without making careless choices you'll later regret.

Success & What it Costs

CHAPTER 11

SEEK GOD & UNDESTANDING

T heologists, scientists, and thought leaders have attempted for centuries to understand the impact that religion can have on human beings; both mentally and physically. And it is commonly accepted around the world that religion and spirituality are among the most important cultural factors—giving structure and meaning to behaviors, value systems, and experiences.

I'm going to be completely and 100% honest. The most

important key to success in life will come from your relationship with the higher power. Now, most people have their own opinion on religion, and everyone is entitled to their opinions. However, facts will always outweigh opinions any day. During my time in prison, I got in some trouble and had to spend 60 days inside the hole. The hole is a 24-hour lockdown inside a cell. Phone calls were once every 30 days, so the only human interaction you had was through mail. You'll never completely understand loneliness until you've experienced being inside the hole. Who do you call out to for help in a time like this? Well, after maybe a few days, I realized I wasn't alone. God was with me the entire time. Reading my bible gave me comfort. This was an eye-opening time in my life because I realized not only was I not alone in this moment, but I was never alone. I've been robbed at gunpoint in the streets, been in shootouts and high speeds, and I'm still here to tell the stories. Please listen when I tell you God is real! Life began to make sense when I began to add God to all my decisions. I realized I have a purpose. I'm a walking testimony. My story will truly change someone's life. When you begin to walk in your purpose, you no longer question things that happen in life, bad or good, because you understand that every moment is a teachable moment. As long as you walk with

God, your life will always be on track. Even in times of Chaos, you'll seek the lesson in those situations. Having a relationship with God brings discipline to your life, and discipline is essential on your journey! Without discipline, you'll be distracted, pulled left and right, and not know what direction to go. God has all the answers. You can take it from me. I am far from perfect; however, I strive to be the best version of myself, and I honestly would not be able to do it without God. He gave me all the words to say in this book, and I believe my words will save someone's life. Understand you are not alone in this world! We make our time harder when we lean on our own understanding. Seek the truth & mark my words; your life will flow 10x more smoothly.

Psalm 1:6: For the LORD watches over the way of the righteous, but the way of the wicked leads to destruction.

CONCLUSIONS

Success takes exactly what it takes – it takes repeating seemingly insignificant actions over time. Without your "why," you have nothing to fight for – it's more than an attitude adjustment; it's defining the philosophy that creates your attitude, which then dictates your actions.

This is why in order to achieve greatness, you must have a winning mindset. It's your "why" that helps you see that the small, tiresome choices you make every day are playing an essential role in your journey toward success. It helps you understand these choices are what dictate whether you fail, survive, or succeed. It also helps you understand that success is incredibly simple because you realize that you already know how to do what it takes to achieve your dreams—those things that helped you survive and got you to where you are today. You'll also understand that success is incredibly difficult because it's just as easy to not be successful and to stop practicing the good habits that started you on your upward trend.

You have the potential to live the life you want, and you have the choice to be a flat-out failure. The person you'll become is under no one's control but your own.

There are no shortcuts to success. The only shortcuts come from your experience. Once you know what to do and how to do it, you will be much more capable of getting things done the fastest way possible. However, this takes time, and success essentially comes down to your ability to use time effectively. This requires that you focus on the right things, at the right time, in the right way, and spend just the right amount of time on them. It's as simple as that; however, it's not simple. It's hard work, and it takes a lot of effort and experience to get things to this stage.

The reality of the matter is that most people are simply not willing to make the necessary sacrifices or to pay the ultimate price for success. This is either good or bad news for you. It's bad news if you're one of these people and not willing to make these sacrifices, however, it's good news if you're not one of these people because it means that you already have the upper hand just from the fact that you are willing to make the necessary sacrifices to attain your goals and objectives.

You'll face many struggles along the way if you are seeking success and happiness. If you are the sower, your seeds will get picked up by the birds first and won't give a return. Then they will fall on shallow ground, leaving you with nothing again. Then they will fall on thorny ground, and the sun will shine so hot that your small plant will die after the first day; no return either. But success comes to those who persevere through trial. The sower that is able to learn from their misfortunes and continue to push forward without getting discouraged will soon reap their harvest.

"Yes, knowledge is power but only potentially. For your research to pay off, you have to do something with it and apply what you've learned. We feel our best when we are moving toward our goals, and it isn't about big steps; it's about consistent steps. That's when we build momentum.

Every winner is a story of dedication. You have a vision? Fix your eyes on the target and be ready to work extremely hard on it. Always remember, there is no feast without a sacrifice.

Nothing is free in life; everything has got a price, and you must be ready to pay it.

CPSIA information can be obtained
at www.ICGtesting.com
Printed in the USA
JSHW051410060323
38507JS00004B/45